asian spice

PUBLISHER'S NOTE

It is with great pleasure that **Ola Editions** is making its debut on the publishing stage with *a*sian *s*pice.

We would like to thank Joan Pereyra for so kindly agreeing to write this book, a first for her as well, and embarking on this venture with us. This book has reached fruition owing much to the advice of Bernice Narayanan, our publishing consultant and the support of family members Sundra, Louis, Priscilla, Alexsy and a very special thanks to the family of the late Mrs MK Dasen.

The very heart of Asian cuisine lies with the delicate balance in the use of spices and condiments. The recipe collection in this book shows you refreshingly innovative ways of preparing well-known favourites with easily available spices and condiments. Conjure up mouth-watering meals and add sparkle to your dining table with the recipes and suggested menus.

We know a truly exotic culinary adventure awaits you and your guests with *a*sian *s*pice and may you have the same pleasure we have had in bringing you this publication.

Ola Editions

preface

"JOAN, how do you cook this dish, can you show me?" It was this sort of question that ultimately led me to decide to compile simple yet tasty recipes into a book. It seemed a daunting task at first, but with the encouragement from family and friends, I have tried to provide a selection of recipes for those who want to entertain and still have fun. The kitchen is the central focus in almost every household and it should be a place for creative culinary experience. Although the recipes provided here are simple, there is no end to the variety with which you could experiment with the spices and condiments should you choose to do so.

Writing this entire book has been a challenging but pleasant experience and it is my sincerest hope that those of you aspiring to entertain with ease will find it easy to follow the recipes I have selected.

Cooking a meal is not a chore but a labour of love and with the modern conveniences available today, it should be an enjoyable experience. To me, there is no greater pleasure than to see my family and friends enjoy food prepared in so many delightful ways.

To those of you who are first time cooks, do not despair as it is not as difficult as you think to prepare a meal all by yourself. I hope this book will be able to help you in more ways than one.

I am indeed glad to be able to share the pleasure of cooking not only a truly authentic Asian meal, but also some traditional Western dishes with a difference.

Joan Pereyra

acknowledgements

IT is with much gratitude that I would like to thank my family and friends for their efforts in helping me to realise my ambition to write this book.

I would like to thank firstly my grandmothers. Though they are no longer around to guide me, it was from them that I learnt to truly appreciate and cook good food - the secret to a good meal lies in the preparation as well as the cooking!

..... my mother, Beryl Pereyra, who has always been encouraging and supportive of whatever I decided to try my hand at (she had the confidence even when I did not). She taught me several of the recipes in the book in particular the Vindaloo recipe (front cover)

..... my mother-in-law whose petite form belies her incredible energy and who taught me that Indian food can be varied to suit any taste.

..... my sisters, Pam and Lyn who sent me recipes, ideas and advice even though we are continents apart.

..... official tasters, critics and creative people, my children , Sharon, Joanne and Kelly for writing, proof reading, typing and supplying me with endless cups of coffee!

..... my husband Louis, a man of a few words but who will travel 250 miles to get home for dinner - a rare compliment indeed.

..... my grandchildren Tracey, Darryl and Sheldon, to them I leave a legacy I hope they will treasure.

......my cousin Ann Jackson and aunt, Edwina Tyson for their recipes and most of all encouragement.

..... my good friend Selva , who is always willing to share cooking tips and recipes with me as well as cook delicious meals for my family. Her recipe Selva's Lamb Chops is an example of her exquisite Indian cuisine.

..... all the people involved in the production of this book especially Primila, Terry and Michael - the photography sessions were an experience I will never forget.

.... to everyone else who has helped in one way or another to make this a successful venture. All of you have my deepest gratitude.

soup

chicken velvet

ingredients

1 cup boiled chicken (shredded)
2 cups water or chicken stock
1 can creamed sweet corn
½ cup crab meat (optional)
1 egg (beaten)
2 tsps light soya sauce
1 tsp chicken granules
2 chinese mushrooms (soaked and sliced)
1 tbsp chopped green onion

method

Put the chicken stock or water in a pan and bring to the boil.
Add the chicken granules and stir.
Then add the sweetcorn, mushrooms, light sauce, salt and pepper.
Cook for about 3 — 5 minutes.
Now stir in the crabmeat and shredded chicken.
Lastly, add the beaten egg.
Remove from heat and garnish with chopped green onions.
Serves 4

opposite page: sweet sour fish fillets (recipe on page 50)

oxtail soup

ingredients

600 gm oxtail (cut into pieces)
1 stalk lemongrass (crushed)
1 big onion (sliced thick)
juice of 1 lime or ½ a lemon
3 — 4 bird eye chillies (crushed)
(optional)
salt
3 — 4 cups water

method

Boil the oxtail in water and salt until the meat is tender.
Add the crushed lemongrass, sliced onion and chillies.
Allow to boil for about 3 — 5 minutes, then add the lime juice.
Remove and serve piping hot
Serves 4

opposite page: cabbage patch stew (recipe on page 54)

stuffed beancurd soup

ingredients

4 pieces beancurd
300 gm minced chicken or pork
2 tomatoes (quartered)
50 gm flat peas
100 gm young corn
1 carrot (cubed)
3 cloves garlic (minced)
1 tsp sesame oil
½ tsp white pepper
½ tbsp light soya sauce
½ tbsp oyster sauce
1 tbsp oil
garnish
chopped spring onions
fried onions

method

Mix the minced meat with the sauces, salt and pepper. Set aside.
Cut the beancurd squares in half diagonally. Scoop out the centre.
Fill the centres with the minced meat mixture. Press it in well.
Fry the minced garlic in 1 tbsp of oil.
Next, add 2 cups of water.
When the water starts to boil, put in the carrots and young corn.
Next, add the beancurd pieces gently.
When these are about to be cooked, add the tomatoes and flat peas.
Cook for a while, then remove from heat.
Garnish and dribble with sesame oil.
Serve piping hot.
Serves 4 — 6

pork-ball soup

ingredients

300 gm minced pork
2 cups water or stock
½ small carrot (cubed)
2 squares beancurd (cubed)
2 cloves garlic (minced)
2 tsps light soya sauce
1 tsp sesame oil
1 tsp cornflour
1 tbsp chopped green onions
1 tbsp fried onions
1 tbsp oil
salt and pepper to taste

method

Fry the minced garlic in 1 tbsp oil.
Add the 2 cups of water or stock.
Mix the minced pork with the light soya sauce, pepper, salt, sesame oil and 1 tbsp cornflour.
Form into small balls.
When the water is boiling, drop the pork balls in.
Add the carrots and beancurd.
When carrots are cooked, add some salt and pepper to the soup.
Remove and sprinkle with chopped green onions and fried onions.
Serves 4 — 6

spicy indian soup

ingredients

600 gm shredded chicken
2 cups water or stock
1 large onion (sliced)
3 cloves garlic (minced)
6 curry leaves
½ tsp ground coriander
½ tsp cracked black pepper
½ tsp cummin
3 cloves
2 cm piece cinnamon
½ cup diluted coconut cream
chopped almonds
1 tbsp oil
salt to taste

method

Fry garlic, onions, coriander, cummin, cloves, cinnamon and curry leaves in a tbsp of oil until fragrant.
Add in the chicken, stir well and pour in the stock or water.
Bring to the boil, then lower heat and gently stir in coconut cream.
Add salt and black pepper.
To serve, pour into bowls and sprinkle with chopped almonds.
Serves 4 — 6

Cook's Tip : Coriander leaves can also be used in place of the almonds.

spicy prawn and beancurd soup

ingredients

2 pieces 8 cm square soft white
beancurd
200 gm shelled prawns
2 stalks spring onions cut into 5 cm
pieces
2 cups water
2 tbsps oil
salt

blend together
2 red chillies (seeded)
2 large onions
1 tsp shrimp powder

method

Cut each beancurd square into 9 pieces.
Fry blended ingredients in hot oil until oil
rises to the top.
Add the shelled prawns.
Next, add 2 cups of water.
When soup starts to boil, add the
beancurd pieces and salt.
After about 5 minutes, add the spring
onions.
Remove from heat and serve.
Serves 4 — 6

Cook's Tip : You can include fishballs for more variety.

beef

beef stew

ingredients

600 gm beef (sliced)
3 potatoes (halved)
1 big onion (quartered)
1 big onion (sliced)
1 carrot (cut into thick slices)
2 tomatoes (quartered)
1 full tbsp breadcrumbs
4 cm piece cinnamon
3 cloves
½ tsp cracked black pepper
5 peppercorns
2 tbsps oil
2 cups water

method

Fry cinnamon, cloves, peppercorns and sliced onions in 2 tbsps oil until onions are soft and slightly brown.
Add the sliced beef and fry well for about 5 minutes.
Then, add the water.
When the meat is half cooked, add the carrots, potatoes and quartered onion.
When potatoes are almost cooked, add the tomatoes, salt and cracked black pepper.
Finally, add the breadcrumbs.
Serve piping hot.
Serves 4 — 6

Cook's Tip : If breadcrumbs are not available, add ½ tsp cornflour.

beef semur

ingredients

600 gm beef (sliced)
3 potatoes (halved)
1 big onion (sliced)
1 big onion (quartered)
1 tsp cracked black pepper
1 tbsp thick soya sauce
1 — 2 tbsp vinegar
1 tbsp light soya sauce
2 cups water
2 tbsps oil

method

Mix the beef with pepper, thick soya sauce and light soya sauce.
Fry sliced onions until soft, then add the beef.
Fry beef for about 5 — 8 minutes then add the water.
When it starts to boil add the potatoes and quartered big onion.
When potatoes are cooked add the vinegar and salt.
Serve hot with rice or bread.
Serves 4 — 6

Cook's Tip : Carrots can be added to sweeten the flavour of the gravy.

eurasian beef steak

ingredients

2 beef steaks
1 tsp cracked black pepper
2 tsps light soya sauce
1 tsp thick soya sauce
2 tsps lime juice
1 tsp cornflour
2 tbsps oil

method

Marinate steaks with all the ingredients.
Leave aside for 10 — 15 minutes.
Fry steaks until brown on each side.
Serve with vegetables and potato chips.
Serves 2

Cook's Tip : Sear steaks well for a minute, then lower heat to prevent the meat from drying.

opposite page: spicy beef rissoles (recipe on page 19)

beef curry

ingredients

600 gm beef (cubed)
3 potatoes (quartered)
1 cup coconut cream
2 tbsps curry powder
2 big onions (sliced fine)
3 cm piece fresh ginger (sliced fine)
4 cloves garlic (sliced fine)
5 curry leaves
juice of one lime or ½ a lemon
3 cm piece cinnamon
2 cloves
2 cups water
salt to taste
2 tbsps oil

method

Mix the curry powder with about ½ cup of water and set aside.
Fry cinnamon and cloves in 2 tbsps of oil, then add the sliced onion, garlic, ginger and curry leaves.
When onions are soft and slightly brown, add the curry powder paste. Fry the spice well until oil comes to the top.
Now add the meat and stir well.
Lower heat and cover for about 10 minutes.
Then, add the potatoes and 2 cups of water.
Cover and cook until meat is tender and potatoes are cooked.
Add the coconut cream, lime juice and salt. Stir well.
Cook uncovered, stirring all the time for another 5 — 10 minutes.
Serve with rice or bread.
Serves 4 — 6

Cook's Tip : When adding in the coconut milk, keep stirring to prevent it from curdling.

spicy beef rissoles

ingredients

600 gm minced beef
1 level tsp chilli powder
1 level tbsp curry powder
1 big onion (chopped)
2 cm piece ginger (chopped fine)
5 curry leaves (chopped)
1 green chilli (seeded and chopped
1 egg (beaten)
salt to taste
$^1/_2$ cup oil

method

Mix all the ingredients together.
Keep mixing well until all the ingredients
are well combined.
Form into balls about the size of a wal-
nut, then flatten a little.
Deep fry until golden brown.
Serves 4 — 6

Cook's Tip : When shaping the mixture into balls, press firmly and roll it around in the palm of your hand to prevent it from crumbling.

kofta curry

ingredients

400 gm minced beef
3 potatoes (quartered)
1½ tbsps curry powder
1 big onion (sliced fine)
3 cloves garlic (sliced fine)
2 cm piece fresh ginger (shredded)
4 curry leaves
½ cup coconut cream
1½ cups water
2 tbsps oil
salt and pepper to taste

method

Mix the minced beef with the pepper, salt and 1 tsp of the curry powder.
Make meat balls with the mixture. Press well to form firm balls.
Fry the sliced onions, garlic and shredded ginger in hot oil.
When onions are soft and slightly brown, add the curry powder and ¼ cup of the water.
Fry the spice well until the oil rises to the top, then add the potatoes and 1½ cups of water. When the curry starts to boil, add the meat balls. Add coconut cream and salt when the potatoes and meatballs are cooked.
Cook for another 5 — 8 minutes then remove and serve with hot rice or bread.
Serves 4 — 6

Cook's Tip : Minced pork or prawns can also be used to cook this curry.

stir fried black pepper beef

ingredients

400 gm beef fillet (sliced fine)
1 green pepper (seeded and cut into cubes)
2 green onions (cut into 4 cm lengths)
1 big onion (quartered)
1 red chilli (seeded and sliced thick)
1 tsp cracked black pepper
1 tbsp cornflour
2 cm piece ginger (shredded)
2 cloves garlic (minced)
1 tbsp light soya sauce
salt to taste
2 tbsps oil

method

Mix beef with soya sauce, pepper and cornflour. Set aside.
Fry minced garlic and ginger.
Add the seasoned meat and stir fry quickly.
Put in the onion, green pepper, chilli and green onion.
Add salt and stir well.
Serve at once.
Serves 4

Cook's Tip : Ingredients in stir fried dishes should be cooked over high heat very quickly as they lose their texture otherwise.

dry liver curry

ingredients

1 kg beef liver (cubed)
2 onions (sliced fine)
4 cm piece ginger (shredded)
4 cloves garlic (minced)
5 curry leaves
½ cup coconut cream
1 tbsp curry powder
½ tbsp chilli powder
1 level tsp turmeric powder
3 green chillies (sliced thick)
2 tbsps oil
lime juice (optional)
salt to taste

method

In a frying pan heat oil, then add sliced onions, shredded ginger, minced garlic and curry leaves. Fry well until onions are slightly brown.

Mix the chilli powder, curry powder and turmeric powder together with ½ cup water to form a paste.

Add the curry paste to the fried ingredients, fry until fragrant and the oil rises to the top.

Next, add the cubed liver and keep stirring well.

Add the salt and coconut cream and keep stirring.

Lastly, add the lime juice and sliced green chillies.

Stir and remove from heat.

Serves 6 — 8

Cook's Tip : Do not overcook the liver as it will be tough.

opposite page: asian pork chop (recipe on page 60)

chicken

ma's devil curry

ingredients

1 kg chicken (cut into bite-sized pieces)
3 potatoes (peeled and cut into wedges)
1 cup water
2 — 3 tbsps vinegar
2 tbsps oil
salt to taste

blend together

2 big onions
12 fresh red chillies (seeded)
1½ cm piece ginger
2 level tsps mustard powder
5 cloves garlic

slice fine

1 red chilli
2 cm piece ginger
1 big onion

method

Fry the sliced onion, chilli and ginger in hot oil. Add the blended ingredients and fry until fragrant and oil rises to the top.
Add chicken pieces and stir well.
Put in potato wedges and 1 cup water.
Cover and lower heat.
After about 5 minutes, remove cover and mix well.
When potatoes and chicken are cooked, add vinegar and salt.
Serve with hot white rice or bread.
Serves 4 — 5

opposite page: vegetable coconut curry (recipe on page 77)

vindaloo

ingredients

1 kg chicken (cut into bite-sized pieces)
or 1 kg pork (cubed)
3 potatoes (quartered)
1 cup water
2 — 3 tbsps vinegar
salt to taste
2 tbsps oil
blend together
12 dried chillies
2 big onions
4 cloves garlic
3 cm piece ginger
1 tsp fennel
2 tsps cummin
1 tsp mustard seed

method

Fry blended ingredients until fragrant.
Add chicken pieces.
Mix well, then cover and leave to simmer
for about 5 minutes.
Add potatoes and 1 cup water. Cover.
When chicken and potatoes are cooked,
add salt and vinegar.
Serve with hot white rice.
Serves 4

curry leaf special

ingredients

1 kg chicken (cut into bite-sized pieces)
3 potatoes (peeled and cut into wedges)
1 big onion (sliced)
2 red chillies (seeded and sliced)
6 curry leaves
1 tbsp curry powder
½ tbsp chilli powder
1 small ball tamarind
¼ tsp sugar
salt to taste
½ cup oil

method

Mix tamarind with ¼ cup water and extract juice.

In a bowl, mix together curry powder, chilli powder, salt, sugar and tamarind juice.

Add the chicken and stir until chicken is well coated with the mixture.

Leave to marinate for 20 — 30 minutes.

Fry the potato wedges until cooked and slightly brown. Remove and drain.

Fry the chicken pieces until cooked. Remove and set aside.

Fry sliced onions, red chillies and curry leaves until soft.

Add the fried chicken and potatoes. Mix well.

Remove and garnish with coriander leaves.

Serves 4

Cook's Tip : Lime or lemon juice may be substituted for tamarind juice.
Juice of ½ lemon is equivalent to 1 tbsp tamarind juice.

tasty nyonya chicken

ingredients

1 kg chicken (cut into bite-sized pieces)
3 potatoes (quartered)
8 shallots (pounded)
5 cloves garlic (minced)
1 full tbsp salted soya bean paste
2 tbsps thick soya sauce
1 level tbsp sugar
2 cups water
3 tbsps oil

method

Heat oil and fry garlic, shallots and soya bean paste.
Add 1 tbsp water.
When fragrant, put in chicken pieces and potatoes. Add 2 tbsps thick soya sauce.
Mix well then add 2 cups water and 1 tbsp sugar.
Cover, lower heat and cook until chicken is tender and gravy is thick.
Serves 4

Cook's Tip : When using salted soya beans, rinse well under running water to remove excess salt and grime.

asian spice

grilled chicken

ingredients

1 kg of chicken (cut into fairly large pieces)
1 level tbsp chilli powder
1 tbsp light sauce
2 tbsps lime juice
1 tbsp oil
1 tsp cracked pepper
salt to taste

method

Marinate the chicken pieces with all the ingredients and set aside for about an hour.
Grill the pieces in an oven toaster or open grill until well cooked.
Serve with a salad.
Serves 4

Cook's Tip : The chicken can be pan fried instead of grilled.

grilled satay chicken

ingredients

1 kg chicken (cut into bite-sized pieces)
½ cup thick coconut milk or coconut cream
1 cup thin coconut milk or diluted coconut cream
salt to taste
sprigs of parsley for garnishing
3 tbsps oil

blend together

6 shallots
6 fresh red chillies
8 dried chillies
3 cm piece fresh turmeric or 1 tsp turmeric powder
2 stalks lemongrass
6 slices galangal
4 candlenuts
1 tsp shrimp paste powder

method

Mix the ground spice, salt and 2 tbsps thick coconut milk together. Marinate the chicken with the ground ingredients and leave to stand for half an hour.
Heat 3 tbsps of oil in a pan and fry the chicken pieces.
Add the thin coconut milk and cook slowly over low heat until chicken is tender. Add the remaining thick coconut milk and cook for about 5 minutes. Dish out and garnish with sprigs of parsley.
Serves 4

Cook's Tip : To grill, add coconut milk to the spice mixture and coat chicken well.

opposite page: chinatown classic (recipe on page 93)

chicken fly by

ingredients

15 chicken wings
marinade
1 tbsp light soya sauce
1 tbsp oyster sauce
1 tbsp thick soya sauce
1 tbsp chilli sauce
1 tbsp tomato sauce
1 tbsp ginger juice
pepper and salt to taste
1 tbsp oil

method

Clean the chicken wings and make slits under the wings.
Mix the wings with the marinade and leave aside for about 30 minutes.
Wrap the wings in foil and grill in an oven toaster or any grill for about 30 minutes.
Remove from foil and garnish.
Serves 5

Cook's Tip : This dish should be served immediately after cooking.

opposite page: stir fired mixed vegetables (recipe on page 84)

white stew

ingredients

1.5 kg chicken (cut into fairly large pieces)
4 potatoes (quartered)
12 shallots or 3 big onions (sliced)
4 green chillies (seeded and halved)
2 cm piece ginger (sliced fine)
5 — 6 curry leaves
4 cm piece cinnamon
1 tsp mustard seed
½ tbsp sugar
1 tbsp vinegar
1 tbsp rice flour or wheat flour
1 tbsp oil or ghee
1 cup coconut cream
2 cups diluted coconut cream
salt to taste

method

In a pan heat oil or ghee and fry the green chillies, ginger, mustard seed, half the sliced onions and curry leaves.
Fry until onions start to brown.
Next, add the chicken pieces and fry for about 5 — 6 minutes.
Then, add the diluted coconut milk and potatoes.
Allow the chicken and potatoes to cook.
Add the coconut cream mixed with the rice flour.
Add the vinegar and stir well.
Remove from heat after adding salt.
In a separate pan, fry the cinnamon and the rest of the sliced onions in a tbsp of oil or ghee.
When the onions are brown, add to the cooked stew.
Serve hot.
Served 6

Cook's Tip : Diluted coconut cream is ½ coconut cream mixed with ½ cup water.

east west roast chicken

ingredients

1 chicken (1.5 kg)
6 potatoes
3 medium-sized onions
2 tbsps butter or margarine

marinade

1 tbsp thick soya sauce
1 tbsp light soya sauce
1 tsp cracked black pepper
1 tsp mustard powder
1½ tsps sugar
1½ tbsps vinegar
salt to taste

method

Clean the chicken well, then mix with the marinade.
Rub the marinade inside the chicken and on the skin.
Leave aside for 15 — 20 minutes.
Put chicken into a roasting pan, then rub butter or margarine all over it.
Put the potatoes in the same pan and dot with butter.
Cover and roast for 40 minutes.
Remove cover and roast for another 5 — 10 minutes.
Carve and serve.
Serves 6

Cook's Tip : Serve with a light white wine.

joan's spicy spring chicken

ingredients

2 spring chickens or 1 large chicken (1.5 kg)
6 tomatoes (chopped)
5 cm piece ginger (ground)
12 fresh red chillies (seeded and ground)
1 tsp turmeric
1 tbsp sugar
2 tbsps tomato sauce
6 cherry tomatoes
1 cup oil
mint for garnishing

method

Clean the chicken well, then rub the ground ginger, salt and turmeric all over it. Leave aside for about 15 minutes. Next, fry the chicken until slightly brown and remove from heat. Set aside.
Remove half the oil from the pan, then put in the ground chilli and fry well.
Add the chopped tomatoes and cook until very soft, stirring all the time.
Next, add the tomato sauce and fried chicken. Mix well, covering the chicken with the spice.
Add the salt and sugar and keep stirring well.
Lastly, add the cherry tomatoes and remove from heat.
Serve garnished with sprigs of mint.
Serves 6

opposite page: selva's lamb chops (recipe on page 42)

lamb

poppyseed curry

ingredients

600 gm lamb
500 ml coconut milk or
diluted coconut cream
1 lime
1 cup water
blend together
2 tbsps poppyseed
1 tsp cummin
½ tsp anise
3 cm piece cinnamon
½ tsp nutmeg powder
4 cloves garlic
4 cm piece ginger
8 dried chillies (soaked and drained)
1 tsp turmeric powder
3 large onions
2 tbsps oil

slice fine
1 large onion
2 red chillies (lengthwise)

method

Fry the ground ingredients in hot oil until fragrant and oil comes to the top.
Add the meat and half of the coconut milk together with 1 cup of water.
Leave to boil, stirring now and then.
Lower heat and simmer until meat is tender.
Now add the rest of the coconut milk.
When it is boiling, add the lime juice and salt.
Add the sliced onions and red chillies.
Cook for a while, then remove from heat.
Serves 4

maharaja lamb

ingredients

1 kg lamb (cubed)
4 potatoes (quartered)
½ cup coconut (fried and ground fine)
1½ cups coconut cream
2 big onions (quartered and sliced fine)
4 cloves garlic (sliced fine)
4 cm piece ginger (shredded)
4 green chillies (sliced)
2 tbsps curry powder
3 cm piece cinnamon
2 cloves
2 cardamons
5 curry leaves
3 tbsps oil
salt to taste

method

Fry cinnamon, cardamons and cloves in hot oil. Add the sliced onions, garlic and ginger.
Fry until onions are slightly brown.
Then, add the curry powder mixed with ½ cup of water and the curry leaves.
Fry this spice well until fragrant and oil comes to the top.
Keep stirring until lamb is well coated with the spice. Lower heat and leave for about 5 minutes.
Stir and add 2 cups of water.
When lamb is half cooked, put in the potatoes. Stir and cover. Allow to simmer until potatoes and lamb are well cooked.
Now, add the coconut cream and salt.
When the gravy is thick, spoon in the fried coconut and sliced green chillies.
Mix this well and continue to cook for about 5 — 7 minutes.
Serve with rice or bread.
Serves 4 — 6

Cook's Tip : This curry keeps well and can be cooked ahead and frozen.
It should be quite dark in colour when cooked.

ann's roast spiced lamb

ingredients

1½ kg shoulder or leg of lamb
1 tsp chilli powder
1 tsp turmeric powder
2 tsps ground coriander
½ tsp fennel
½ tsp cummin
2 cloves garlic (crushed)
2 cm piece ginger (crushed)
1 cup yoghurt

method

Bone the lamb and mix all spices, garlic and ginger with yoghurt and pour over lamb.
Marinate for at least 2 hours or overnight.
Heat oven to moderate level (175 degrees Celcius).
Roll lamb and tie, place in the centre of a baking tray.
Scrape remaining marinade over lamb.
Bake till done (approximately 1½ — 2 hours).
Serves 6 — 8

lamb chop stew

ingredients

600 gm lamb chops
1 cube beef seasoning
1 tbsp oyster sauce
1 tbsp sesame oil
1 tsp cracked black pepper
salt to taste
5 — 6 dried mushrooms (soaked and sliced)
½ tsp dried orange peel (sliced fine)
3 cm piece ginger (sliced fine)
2 tsps light soya sauce
2 tbsps cooking wine (optional)
1 large cup water
2 tbsps cooking oil

method

Cut meat into cubes and marinate with the seasoning, oyster sauce, sesame oil, pepper and salt.
Leave aside for ½ an hour.
Heat oil and put in meat.
Keep stirring, allowing meat to brown slightly.
Next, add sliced ginger, orange peel and light soya sauce.
Add water and allow to cook.
When the meat is tender, add the sliced mushrooms, wine and salt to taste.
Serves 4

Cook's Tip : For a richer stew, add ½ cup milk

selva's lamb chops

ingredients

8 lamb chops
3 potatoes (cut into wedges)
4 tomatoes
5 — 6 curry leaves
2 big onions (sliced)
6 cm piece ginger (ground)
8 cloves garlic (minced)
10 shallots (sliced fine)
6 cm piece cinnamon
5 cardamons
5 cloves
1 star anise
1 lime or ½ lemon
½ tbsp anise (dry fried and pounded)
½ tbsp turmeric powder
2 tbsps curry powder
1 tbsp chilli powder
1 tbsp cracked black pepper
2 tbsps oil
garnish
chopped green onions
coriander leaves

method

Mix chops with ginger, garlic and turmeric. Set aside for 30 minutes. Pressure cook the chops until almost tender. Remove from pressure cooker.

Fry sliced shallots, cinnamon, cardamons, cloves, star anise and curry leaves in 2 tbsps of oil.

When the shallots are slightly brown, add the chops, tomatoes, curry powder, chilli powder and pepper.

Add the potatoes. Cook this over low heat. If it is too dry, sprinkle with some water.

When the potatoes are cooked, add the onion rings and ground, dry fried anise.

Lastly, add the juice of the lime according to taste. Mix well.

Top with chopped green onions and coriander leaves.

Serve with rice or bread.

Serves 4

opposite page: ma's devil curry (recipe on page 24) The photograph in the background is of my grandmother Ethel Lawrence's house in Seremban, Malaysia, built in 1929 where I lived for 13 years.

crab curry

ingredients

6 crabs (cleaned and cut in half)
2 big onions (sliced)
6 cloves garlic (sliced)
3 cm piece fresh ginger (shredded)
5 — 6 curry leaves
1 tsp mustard seed
1 tsp fenugreek
2 tbsps curry powder
2 green chillies (seeded and halved)
2 tomatoes (quartered)
1 cup coconut cream
1 small ball tamarind
2 cups water
salt to taste
3 tbsps oil

method

Fry mustard seed and fenugreek in a dry pan until they start to pop.
Then, add 3 tbsps of oil.
When oil is hot, add sliced onions, garlic and shredded ginger.
Fry until onions are soft and slightly brown.
Then, put in curry powder which has been mixed with ½ cup water.
Fry well until oil comes to the top.
Put in the crabs and stir, making sure that all the crabs are well coated with the spice mixture. Add 1 cup water and mix well.
When crabs become red, add the tomatoes and green chillies.
Put in the coconut cream, mixing well.
Add the strained tamarind juice (tamarind mixed with half a cup of water) and salt.
Cook until dry, stirring all the time.
Serve garnished with coriander leaves and sliced red chillies.
Serves 4

opposite page: joan's spicy spring chicken (recipe on page 36)

mackeral fry

ingredients

4 slices mackeral
1 full tsp chilli powder
½ tsp turmeric powder
½ tsp salt
1 tsp lime juice
3 tbsps oil

method

Wash slices of fish, using salt, then drain.
Mix all the ingredients and season the fish with it.
Leave for about 10 minutes.
Fry the pieces of fish until brown on both sides.
Remove and serve garnished with slices of cucumber on a bed of lettuce.
Serves 4

Cook's Tip : Cook fish over medium heat to prevent the spice coating from burning.

dragonboat

ingredients

1 medium pomfret, perch or carp
3 cm piece ginger (sliced fine)
3 cloves garlic (crushed)
1 red chilli (seeded and sliced)
1 medium-sized onion (sliced)
1 tsp soya bean paste (minced)
½ tbsp chinese wine
½ tbsp light soya sauce
1 tsp sesame oil
spring onions (chopped)

method

Clean the fish, but do not cut it into pieces.
Place whole fish on a dish over a porcelain spoon.
On the fish arrange the ginger, onions, garlic, sliced chilli and soya bean paste.
Dribble the soya sauce, chinese wine and sesame oil over the top.
Place in a steamer and steam for 20 — 30 minutes until fish is cooked.
Remove and sprinkle chopped spring onions and sliced chillies over the top.
Serves 2

Cook's Tip : You can also add thin strips of pork or ham to the fish for a subtle change of flavour.

hot and sour fish steaks

ingredients

4 fish steaks
1 full tsp chilli powder
1 level tsp curry powder
one small ball tamarind (mixed with ¼ cup water)
salt to taste
3 tbsps oil

method

Mix the chilli powder, curry powder, salt and tamarind juice and set aside.
Clean the fish and pat dry.
Pour the spice mixture over the fish and mix well.
Leave to stand for about 10 minutes.
Fry the fish pieces until slightly crisp and brown on both sides.
Remove to a plate.
Serve with slices of lemon and potato chips.
Serves 4

Cook's Tip : Wash fish with coarse salt to remove slime.

opposite page: vindaloo (recipe on page 26)
We would like to thank the family of the late Mrs M K Dasen
for the exquisite antique brassware in the photograph.

sweet sour fish fillets

ingredients

2 medium bream, perch or hake fillets
1 small cucumber (cubed)
½ green pepper (cubed)
½ small tin pineapple cubes
3 pips garlic (crushed)
1 onion (sliced)
1 red chilli (seeded and sliced thick)
2 tbsps tomato sauce
1 tbsp chilli sauce
1 tbsp light soya sauce
½ tbsp vinegar
1 tsp sugar
1 tsp cornflour
¼ cup water
salt to taste
3 tbsps oil

method

Clean the fish fillets and season with salt.
Deep fry fish until golden brown. Remove to a plate.
Fry crushed garlic in a little oil, then add sliced onion, cubed cucumber, pineapple, green pepper and tomato.
Pour in the sauces and bring to a boil.
Then, add the cornflour mixed with ¼ cup water.
When mixture has thickened, pour over fish and serve at once.
Serves 2

golden hardtails

ingredients

4 hardtails
$^1/_2$ cup oil
spices to blend
12 dried chillies
1 big onion
1 tsp shrimp powder

method

Clean the fish, but do not remove the hard skin.
Slit the backs above the bone.
Wash the fish with salt water.
Drain and pat dry.
Mix the blended spice with 1 level tsp salt and rub the spice all over the fish inside and out and into the slit backs.
Deep fry the fish until the edges are crisp and brown.
Serve with slices of lemon.
Serves 4

deep sea spicy prawns

ingredients

18 large prawns
1 cup oil for deep frying
mix together
1 tbsp curry powder
1 tsp chilli powder
½ tsp salt
1 tsp chicken granules
4 curry leaves
1 small ball tamarind
(mixed with ¼ cup water)
garnish
lettuce leaves
sliced cucumber
sliced tomatoes

method

Clean prawns, remove head and devein, but leave unshelled.
Mix the prawns with all the ingredients and leave aside for 20 minutes.
Heat oil and deep fry, but do not over-cook.
Place on a flat serving platter and garnish.
Serves 6

Cook's Tip : Leave the prawn with its skin and tail intact to prevent it from shrinking during cooking.

indian prawn curry

ingredients

12 large prawns
1 eggplant (sliced into 3 cm pieces)
2 tomatoes (quartered)
2 green chillies (halved lengthwise)
2 large onions (sliced)
3 cm piece ginger (shredded)
4 cloves garlic (minced)
4 curry leaves
1 tbsp full curry powder
1 tsp full chilli powder
1 small ball tamarind
(mixed with ½ cup water)
½ cup coconut cream
½ tsp mustard seed
½ tsp fenugreek
2 tbsps oil

method

Dry fry mustard seed and fenugreek.
Add the oil and fry the sliced onions,
ginger, garlic and curry leaves until
onions start to brown.
Add the curry powder, chilli powder and
½ cup water.
Fry the spice well until fragrant, and oil
rises to the top.
Then, add the eggplant pieces and stir
well.
Add the prawns. When prawns and
eggplant are almost cooked, add the
coconut cream and tamarind juice.
When it starts to boil, add the green
chillies and tomatoes.
Cook for about 5 minutes, then remove
from heat.
Serve with hot white rice.
Serves 4

pork

cabbage patch stew

ingredients

400 gm minced pork
2 — 3 potatoes (quartered)
1 onion (sliced)
2 tomatoes (quartered)
3 cm piece cinnamon
3 cloves
5 peppercorns
½ tbsp light soya sauce
½ tbsp oyster sauce
1 tbsp sesame oil
12 cabbage leaves
(blanched in hot water)
2 cups water
salt and pepper to taste
2 tbsps oil

method

Mix the minced pork with the pepper, light soya sauce, oyster sauce, sesame oil and a little salt.
Using the cabbage leaves, make little packets using the meat as a filling.
Tie the packets with some thread or tuck the edges under. Keep the packets aside.
Fry the cinnamon, cloves, pepper corns and sliced onions in hot oil.
Then add the water and potatoes.
When the water starts to boil and the potatoes are semi-cooked, add the cabbage packets gently.
Add the quartered tomatoes.
Serves 2

Cook's Tip : This stew can be thickened by adding 1 tbsp of flour mixed with a little water.

opposite page: ann's roast spiced lamb (recipe on page 40)

empress steamed pork

ingredients

600 gm minced pork
1 big onion (minced)
3 cloves garlic (minced)
1 red chilli (seeded and chopped fine)
2 spring onions (chopped fine)
2 eggs (beaten)
½ cup water
1 tbsp oyster sauce
1 tsp sesame oil
salt and pepper
fried onions

method

Place the minced meat, onion, garlic, chopped chilli, eggs, water, salt, pepper, oyster sauce, sesame oil and half the chopped spring onions together in a bowl. Mix well.

Place in a greased dish and press firmly. Steam until skewer comes out clean. When cooked, remove from heat and sprinkle the top with the remaining chopped spring onions and sliced chillies.

Cut into pieces to serve.

Serves 4

Cook's Tip : Recommended for children without chillies.

opposite page: silver and gold (recipe on page 70)

oriental grill

ingredients

600 gm streaky pork
(cut into 3 pieces lengthwise)
cucumber
tomatoes
lettuce
marinade
1 tsp white pepper
1 tbsp light sauce
2 tbsps Hoisin sauce
½ tbsp oil

method

Mix the 3 pieces of pork with the marinade and leave to stand for 20 minutes.
Grill the pieces of pork, turning every 10 minutes.
When pork is well grilled, remove and slice.
Serve on a bed of lettuce with sliced tomatoes and cucumber.
Serves 4

Cook's Tip : Serve with a hot garlic sauce.

beryl's rissoles

ingredients

600 gm minced pork
3 potatoes (boiled, skinned and mashed)
1 small egg (beaten)
pepper and salt
bread crumbs
3 tbsps oil

method

Combine the minced pork, mashed potatoes, salt, pepper and beaten egg. Mix well and from into patties. Flatten and round the patties.

Dip in bread crumbs and fry in a non-stick frying pan until brown on both sides.

Serve on platter with sliced cucumber and tomatoes.

Serves 4

Cook's Tip : To keep patties from crumbling, add ½ tsp cornflour to the mixture.

asian pork chop

ingredients

6 pieces pork chop
marinade
1 tsp ground black pepper
½ tbsp light soya sauce
1 tbsp thick soya sauce
1 tbsp lime juice
½ tbsp cornflour
salt to taste
3 tbsps oil
1 big onion (sliced)
2 tomatoes (sliced)
½ cup green peas

method

Mix the chops with the marinade. Coat well and leave to stand for 10 minutes.
Fry the chops until brown on both sides and meat is cooked.
Remove to a plate.
Fry the sliced onions and add the tomatoes.
Add the green peas.
Pour over the chops.
Serves 4

Cook's Tip : Can be served with potato salad or coleslaw as well.

coriander meat strips

ingredients

600 gm streaky pork
(sliced into thin strips)
6 cloves garlic (minced fine)
1 tsp coriander powder
1 small ball tamarind (mix with ½ cup
water and extract juice)
1 tbsp white vinegar
1 tbsp thick soya sauce
2 — 3 whole red chillies
1 level tbsp sugar
1 tbsp oil

method

Fry the minced garlic in oil, and then add
the coriander powder.
Add the sliced meat and stir well. Fry
until oil rises to the top.
Then add the tamarind juice and vinegar.
Stir well in pan and add the thick soya
sauce, sugar and whole red chillies.
Keep frying until the meat is shiny in
appearance.
Remove from heat and serve.
Serves 4

Cook's Tip : Fresh coriander can be used as a garnish.

spare ribs special

ingredients

1½ kg spare ribs
(cut into small pieces)
marinade
3 tbsps light soya sauce
2 tbsps honey
1 tsp sugar
3 tbsps Hoisin sauce
1 tbsp chinese wine
½ tsp five spice powder
2 tbsps white vinegar
1 onion (chopped fine)
salt to taste
1 tbsp oil

method

Mix the ribs well with the marinade and leave in the refrigerator for a few hours.
Heat grill.
Place spare ribs on an oiled wire rack in a roasting pan.
Add some water to the roasting pan to prevent burning.
Grill for 20 — 30 minutes,
basting with oil.
Turn once or twice.
When done, garnish and serve.
Serves 6

Cook's Tip : Ribs can also be barbequed or pan-fried.

opposite page: east west roast chicken (recipe on page 35)

ginger pork

ingredients

500 gm lean pork
2 potatoes (halved and sliced)
2 tomatoes (quartered)
1 medium-sized onion (sliced)
4 cm piece ginger (sliced fine)
1 small bunch garlic chives or spring
onions (cut into 3cm lengths)
½ tbsp light soya sauce
1 tsp thick soya sauce
1 tbsp oyster sauce
1 tbsp oil
pepper and salt to taste

method

Heat the oil in a frying pan or wok and fry
ginger and onions well.
Then add the sliced pork and stir well.
After a while, add the potato slices.
Add the thick soya sauce, light soya
sauce, oyster sauce and 1 cup water.
Cover and allow to cook until potatoes
are soft, then add pepper.
Add the tomatoes.
Lastly, add spring onions or garlic chives
and remove from heat.
Serves 4

Cook's Tip : This dish can also be cooked with chicken.

opposite page: kofta curry (recipe on page 20),
eastern savoury rice (recipe on page 85), eggplant pickle (recipe on page 76)

tamarind tryout

ingredients

600 gm belly pork (cubed)
1 small ball tamarind mixed with ½ cup water (strained)
5 cloves garlic (minced)
2 — 3 red chillies (sliced thickly)
1 tsp sugar
1 tbsp light soya sauce
1 tbsp thick soya sauce
salt to taste

method

Place the pork slices in a hot wok without any oil.
Stir fry until brown on both sides. The oil will seep out of the meat. Lower heat if it is too hot.
Remove from pan and set aside.
In the same wok, remove some of the oil if it is too much. Fry minced garlic and chillies.
Then add fried pork, light soya sauce, thick soya sauce, tamarind water, sugar and salt.
Fry well.
Remove and garnish.
Serves 4

Cook's Tip : This dish should be cooked quickly over high heat.

egg curry

ingredients

6 hardboiled eggs
6 shallots (sliced) or 1 large onion (sliced)
1 tbsp curry powder
2 cm piece ginger (sliced fine)
3 cloves garlic (sliced fine)
3 — 4 curry leaves
1 cup coconut milk/coconut cream
3 potatoes (boiled and skinned)
½ cup water
salt to taste
2 tbsps oil
coriander leaves for garnishing

method

Heat the oil in a saucepan.
Fry the onions, curry leaves, ginger and garlic until soft.
Add the curry powder which has been mixed to a paste with a little water.
Fry until fragrant. Add the coconut milk and water and bring slowly to the boil.
Add the whole hard boiled eggs and boiled potatoes which have been quartered.
Cook gently for 5 minutes. Add salt to taste.
Dish out and garnish with coriander leaves.
Serves 4

Cook's Tip : When hard boiling eggs, do not boil for more than 8 minutes to prevent grey rings from forming around the yolks.

asian omelette

ingredients

4 eggs
1 large onion (chopped)
1 red chilli (chopped)
1 green chilli (chopped)
½ carrot (grated)
1 chinese sausage (cut into thin slices)
2 tbsps water
salt and pepper to taste
chinese parsley for garnishing

method

Beat the eggs and add 2 tbsps of water.
Fry the chopped ingredients in 2 tbsps of oil.
Add the sliced chinese sausage and grated carrot.
Pour the egg mixture over and lower heat.
Cook gently until the mixture is firm.
Turn over and cook the other side.
Serve hot garnished with chopped chinese parsley.
Serves 2

Cook's tip : Chinese sausages have a thin, transparent outer skin which should be removed.

egg sambal*

ingredients

6 hard boiled eggs (pricked)
1 cup oil
2 tbsps tomato sauce
1 tsp sugar
1 cup water
1 cup green peas
salt to taste
2 tbsps oil
blend together
12 dried chillies
8 shallots or 2 big onions
4 cloves garlic
2 cm piece ginger

* a combination of chillies and spices which normally accompanies rice and curry meals

method

Heat the oil and fry eggs until slightly brown. Remove onto plate.
Fry the ground spice until fragrant and well cooked.
Add the water, tomato sauce and sugar.
When the mixture is boiling, add the fried hard boiled eggs and stir.
Add the green peas and remove from heat.
Dish out and serve garnished with sliced chillies and chopped coriander leaves.
Serves 4

silver and gold

ingredients

300 gm fish (mackerel)
1 tsp cornflour
6 tsps salt water (1 level tsp salt and water)
2 tbsps oil
pepper and salt to taste
garnishing
lettuce
red chillies
omelette
4 eggs
2 tbsps water

method

Beat the eggs lightly with a fork. Add salt, pepper and 2 tbsps water.
Heat a pan and grease well. Fry the eggs into 4 thin omelettes. Dish out and leave to cool on a plate.
Wash, slice and scrape flesh of fish from skin.
Pound well. Add very gradually the 6 tsps of salt water while pounding.
When the mixture is quite fine, add the pepper and cornflour.
Mix well and spread mixture evenly on the omelettes.
Roll up and steam the egg rolls in a steamer. Serve the egg roll cut into thin slices with chilli sauce.
Serves 2

Cook's Tip : Chopped prawns can be added to the fish mixture.

opposite page: crab curry (recipe on page 44)

vegetables

peanut sauce salad

ingredients

300 gm beansprouts (cleaned and blanched)
1 turnip (sliced into thin strips)
1 cucumber (sliced into thin strips)
2 hardboiled eggs (quartered)
300 gm water convolvulus (cleaned and blanched)
2 beancurd squares (fried and sliced)
½ small pineapple (cubed)
8 green beans
150 gm roasted peanuts (chopped fine) or 1 tbsp chunky peanut butter
1 small ball tamarind (mix with 1 cup water)
sugar to taste
2 tbsps oil
salt to taste

blend together (for gravy)
15 dried chillies
10 shallots or 2 big onions

method

In hot oil, fry the ground ingredients until fragrant.
Add the roasted chopped peanuts or peanut butter.
Fry well, then add the tamarind juice and sugar.
Cook for about 10 minutes. Add salt to taste.
To serve place vegetables, hard boiled eggs and beancurd squares on a plate.
Pour gravy over generously.
Serves 2 — 3

opposite page: spare ribs special (recipe on page 62)

spicy potatoes

ingredients

4 large potatoes (peeled and cut into cubes)
1 large onion (sliced fine)
2 dried chillies (broken into pieces)
5 curry leaves
1 level tsp turmeric powder
1 level tbsp curry powder
3 tbsps oil
salt to taste

method

Mix the potatoes with the salt, turmeric and curry powder and set aside.
Fry the potatoes in hot oil until cooked and slighty brown. Remove and drain.
Add 1 tbsp oil and fry the sliced onions, dried chillies and curry leaves.
Add the fried potatoes and mix well.
Remove and serve.
Serves 2

Cook's Tip: For variety, you can add a can of chick peas to this potato dish.
It makes a very good vegetarian dish and is a big hit.

vegetarian special

ingredients

2 medium eggplants (cut into bite-sized pieces)
2 zucchinis (cut in half and sliced) (optional)
10 french beans (sliced)
1 large onion (halved and sliced)
2 semi-ripe tomatoes (quartered)
2 tbsps of oil
1 — 2 tbsps vinegar
1 tsp sugar
1 tbsp light soya sauce
salt to taste

spices to blend

5 dried chillies (soaked and drained)
5 shallots
1 tsp cummin powder
½ tsp anise powder

1½ cm piece ginger
3 cloves garlic
½ tsp mustard powder

method

Fry the eggplants in oil, until soft. Remove and drain. In the remaining oil fry the ground spice. Lower heat to fry the spice well.

When spice is cooked, add onions, zucchinis, french beans and tomatoes. Mix well and cook for a while.

Next, add fried eggplants, light sauce, sugar and vinegar.

Mix well and dish out.

Serves 4

eggplant pickle

ingredients

5 eggplants (sliced into rounds)
salt and turmeric powder to season
eggplant slices
2 tbsps vinegar
1 tbsp sugar
3 tbsps water
salt to taste
2 tbsps oil

spices to blend

12 dried chillies (seeded and soaked)
8 shallots or 2 medium-sized onions
4 cloves garlic
3 cm piece ginger
1½ tsp cummin powder
¾ tsp fennel powder
½ tsp mustard powder

method

Season eggplant slices with the salt and turmeric. Rub it in well and leave for about 10 minutes.

Fry the eggplant slices in hot oil until brown on both sides. Remove to a plate.

Fry the ground ingredients until fragrant then add the water, vinegar, salt and sugar.

Boil until mixture is thick and oil rises to the top.

Spoon cooked mixture over the eggplant slices which have been arranged in a dish.

Serves 4

Cook's Tip : This dish can be made ahead of time and frozen.
It tastes just as good when reheated.

vegetable coconut curry

ingredients

400 gm sweet potato (cleaned and cut into cubes)
400 gm spinach
400 gm water convolvulus
300 gm prawns (shelled)
2 cups prawn stock/water
1 cup coconut cream
2 — 3 pieces dried tamarind
2 tbsps oil

spices to blend

3 red chillies or dried chillies
6 shallots or 1 big onion
1 tsp shrimp powder (optional)
1 dsp dried shrimp (optional)

method

Fry the ground ingredients until fragrant.
Add the prawns and fry well.
Add the prawn stock or water. Bring to the boil and add the sweet potato.
When sweet potato is almost cooked, add the spinach and water convolvulus.
Finally, add the coconut cream and dried tamarind.
Keep stirring and turn off heat when gravy starts to boil.
Serves 4

indian potato salad

ingredients

4 potatoes (peeled and cut into small cubes)
1 carrot (cleaned and cut into cubes)
½ cup green peas
1 tomato (cubed)
1 onion (quartered and sliced)
3 — 4 curry leaves
1 red chilli (seeded and sliced)
1 green chilli (seeded and sliced)
2 dried chillies (broken into 4 pieces)
½ tsp turmeric powder
salt to taste
2 tbsps oil

method

Boil the potatoes and carrots in water until soft.
Add salt and turmeric powder to this.
In another pan fry the onions, curry leaves, red chillies and green chilli.
Pour in the potato and carrot mixture and mix well.
Next, add the tomatoes and the green peas.
Cook until gravy is fairly thick.
This dish can be served with crusty bread or puri.
Serves 4

Cook's Tip : This dish can also be served with chappatis.

vegetarian lentil curry

ingredients

½ cup lentils
2 eggplants (quartered)
3 potatoes (quartered)
1 carrot (cut into thick slices)
1 radish (cut into thick slices)
3 dried chillies (broken into pieces)
1 onion (sliced)
3 cloves garlic (sliced)
1 red chilli (seeded and halved)
3 cm piece ginger (crushed)
½ tsp mustard seed
½ tsp fenugreek
1 cup coconut cream
1 small ball tamarind (mixed with ½ cup water)
1 cup water
1 tbsp oil

method

Boil the lentils with 2 cups of water and the ginger.
When the lentils are almost cooked add the potatoes, eggplant, carrot and radish.
Add a cup of water and bring to the boil.
When the vegetables are cooked, add the coconut cream, tamarind juice and salt.
In a separate pan fry the mustard seed, fenugreek, sliced onion, garlic, dried chillies and curry leaves until brown.
Pour this into the lentil curry.
Mix well and turn off heat.
Garnish with chinese parsley or fried onions.
Serves 4 — 6

exotic phoenix vegetables

ingredients

150 gm flat peas
½ small cabbage
1 small turnip or yam bean
1 carrot
250 gm prawns (chilled)
250 gm lean pork or chicken (sliced into stripes)
6 pips garlic (minced)
1 tbsp soya bean paste
1 cup button mushrooms
½ cup dried mushrooms (soaked and halved)
20 gm glass vermicelli (soaked in water to soften)
½ cup water
1 tbsp oyster sauce
salt to taste
1 tsp sugar
2 tbsps oil

method

Wash and string flat peas.
Cut the cabbage into fairly large pieces.
Cut the turnip into about 3 cm by 3 cm pieces.
Cut the carrot into slices. You can make some fancy shapes if you like.
In a wok, fry the minced garlic then add the soya bean paste.
Add 1 tbsp water and continue frying the mixture until fragrant. Add the sliced meat, prawns and sugar.
Fry for about 3 — 5 minutes then add the turnip and carrots. Mix well.
Add ½ cup water.
Add the cabbage and all the mushrooms.
Lastly, add the glass vermicelli and the flat peas. Stir well and add oyster sauce and salt to taste.
Serves 4 — 6

opposite page: deep sea spicy prawns (recipe on page 52)

easy eggplant platter

ingredients

3 chinese eggplants (sliced thick)
1 green chilli (sliced)
1 red chilli (sliced)
5 curry leaves (chopped)
1 big onion (sliced)
¾ tbsp vinegar
½ tsp sugar
1 cup coconut cream
1 level tsp turmeric powder
salt to taste
2 tbsps oil

method

Season the eggplant slices with salt and turmeric powder.
Deep fry until golden brown.
Remove and set aside.
Mix all the other ingredients in a bowl.
Add the fried eggplant slices and mix well.
Serves 4

Cook's Tip : This dish goes well with a meat curry dish. Serve with hot, white rice. You can omit the coconut milk if it is too rich.

tomato chutney

ingredients

1 kg tomatoes (remove skin and dice)
4 cm piece cinnamon
2 cloves
3 cardamons
½ cup raisins
½ cup cashew nuts
sugar and salt to taste
2 tbsps oil
blend together
8 shallots
1 clove garlic
20 dried chillies
3 cm piece ginger

method

Fry the cinnamon, cloves and cardamons until fragrant.
Then add the ground spice and fry until the oil rises to the top,.
Next, add the tomatoes, salt and sugar.
Simmer until well cooked.
Lastly, add the raisins and cashew nuts.
Cook for a few minutes.
Remove and leave to cool.
This chutney can be kept in the fridge or freezer and taken out when needed.
Serves 6

stir fried mixed vegetables

ingredients

150 gm cauliflower (florets)
1 green pepper (cut into squares)
1 medium-sized carrot (sliced)
6 chinese mushrooms
50 gm pea pods
100 gm lean pork (sliced)
100 gm prawns (cleaned and deveined)
100 gm young corn
10 button mushrooms
3 cloves garlic (minced)
3 cm piece ginger (sliced fine)
1 tbsp light soya sauce
1 tbsp oyster sauce
½ tsp white pepper
1 tsp cornflour
(mixed with a little water)
8 —10 roasted cashew nuts
2 tbsps oil

method

Heat oil in a wok and fry garlic and ginger until light brown.
Add the pork and prawns.
Fry well then add the chinese mushrooms, carrot, cauliflower and button mushrooms.
Stir for two minutes then add the green pepper and pea pods.
Add the light sauce, oyster sauce and pepper. Stir well and add the cornflour mixture.
Remove and garnish with the cashew nuts.
Serves 4

eastern savoury rice

ingredients

2 cups Basmati rice (washed and drained)
2½ cups coconut milk
2 tbsps margarine or butter
1 tsp chopped garlic
¾ tsp chopped ginger
2 cm piece cinnamon
2 star anise
3 cardamons
½ tsp turmeric powder
salt to taste

garnishing
150 gm toasted almond flakes
150 gm raisins
coriander leaves
sliced red chillies

method

Heat the margarine in a saucepan and fry garlic, ginger, cinnamon, star anise and cardamons.
Add the rice and mix well.
Add the coconut milk, salt and turmeric powder.
Transfer contents to a rice cooker and cook.
Serve garnished with almond flakes, raisins, coriander leaves and chillies.
Serves 4

Cook's Tip : When washing rice, handle gently so that the grains don't break.

moghul tomato rice

ingredients

4 cups rice (washed and drained)
1 cup tomato soup
1 large onion (diced)
2 cm piece fresh ginger (chopped fine)
1 clove garlic (sliced fine)
3½ cups water
3 tbsps butter or margarine
salt to taste

method

Put the butter in a pan and fry garlic until golden brown.
Add onion and ginger.
Add rice and fry, stirring well.
Add tomato soup and water.
Cover pan and cook, stirring now and then.
Lower heat and add salt.
Garnish rice with fried onions and sliced red chillies.
Serves 4 — 6

Cook's Tip : Always use long grain rice for exotic rice dishes as the grains separate better and will not form sticky lumps.

opposite page: stir fried black pepper beef (recipe on page 21)

wok style rice

ingredients

400 gm cooked white rice (cooled)
400 gm chicken (cut into cubes)
200 gm shelled prawns (chopped)
½ cup green peas
2 cm piece cinnamon
4 cloves garlic (minced)
1 level tbsp curry powder
1 tsp salt
2 tbsps light soya sauce
2 tbsps oil
garnish
fried onions
chopped spring onions
1 cucumber (sliced)
1 red chilli (sliced)

method

Mix the meat and prawns with the curry powder and salt. Leave aside for 10 minutes.
Heat 2 tbsps oil in a pan and fry the garlic and cinnamon.
Add the meat and prawns.
Stir fry until meat is cooked. Put in the cooked rice, soya sauce and green peas. Stir well.
Remove to a plate and garnish with fried onions, spring onions, cucumber slices and chillies.
Serves 4

Cook's Tip: A very fine omelette can be sliced and used as garnishing too.

opposite page: emerald sweet rolls (recipe on page 105)

coconut rice

ingredients

4 cups rice (washed and drained)
2 cm piece fresh ginger (chopped fine)
3 cups thin coconut milk or diluted
coconut cream
1 cup thick coconut milk or coconut
cream
3 screwpine leaves
1 tsp salt

* a combination of spices and chillies
which normally accompanies rice and
curry meals

method

Place rice, chopped ginger, screwpine
leaves and thin coconut milk into a rice
cooker.
When almost cooked, add thick coconut
milk and stir.
Serve hot with a curry or sambal*.
Serves 4

stir fried veggie rice

ingredients

400 gm cooked white rice (cooled)
2 cm piece cinnamon
4 cloves garlic (minced)
2 tbsps dessicated coconut
¾ tsp turmeric powder
2 tbsps chopped, toasted cashew nuts/ almond
4 curry leaves
1 green chilli (seeded and chopped)
$1/3$ tsp mustard seed
1 cup frozen mixed vegetables
2 tbsps oil
salt to taste

method

Heat 2 tbsps oil in a pan and fry garlic, cinnamon, nuts, curry leaves, mustard seed and green chilli.
Add the cooked rice, dessicated coconut and turmeric powder.
Stir well, add the frozen mixed vegetables and 2 tbsps water.
Cover and leave for about 2 minutes.
Remove cover, stir well and add salt.
Dish out and garnish.
Serves 2

lyn's noodles

ingredients

600 gm wet noodles or 2 packets dried
noodles
2 pieces fish cake (sliced)
10 fish balls (cut each into 3 pieces)
100 gm pork (sliced fine)
100 gm prawns (shelled)
200 gm mustard green
3 red chillies (sliced)
1 large onion (quartered and sliced)
1 clove garlic (minced)
1 tbsp cornflour mixed with 2 tbsps water
1 tbsp oyster sauce
1 tbsp light soya sauce
1 tbsp thick soya sauce
½ tsp cracked pepper
1 tbsp oil

method

Fry the garlic and onions in 1 tbsp oil.
Then add the pork and prawns and stir
well. Add the fish cake and fish balls.
Then add the cracked pepper, light soya
sauce, thick soya sauce and oyster sauce.
Add 1½ cups water and allow to cook on
a high fire for a few minutes.
Add the vegetables and cornflour mixture
to thicken gravy.
If using wet noodles, mix noodles into the
mixture of meat and vegetables.
Stir well and dish out.
Garnish with slices of fried onions and
chopped spring onions.
If using dried noodles, pour boiling water
over the noodles and leave to soften.
Drain the noodles once it softens.
Arrange on a plate and pour mixture on
the noodles.
Garnish with fried onions and sliced red
chillies.
Serves 4

chinatown classic

ingredients

250 gm minced pork
150 gm prawns (cleaned)
400 gm egg noodles
1 green onion (chopped)
1 tsp chicken granules
2 tsps light soy sauce
1 tsp sesame oil
6 dried mushrooms (soaked and sliced)
5 — 6 lettuce leaves (cut into large pieces)
2 cloves garlic (minced)
600 ml water
salt and pepper to taste

method

Mix the minced meat with the sesame oil, salt, pepper and light soya sauce.
Form meat balls with the mixture, pressing firmly.
Wash the noodles and drain.
Put the water and chicken granules into a saucepan and bring to the boil. Add the meatballs and cook until they float to the top.
Add salt, pepper and some soya sauce to the soup. Next, add the prawns and the lettuce.
Cook for one minute.
Add the noodles and remove from heat.
When serving, add the chopped green onion.
Serves 2— 4

Cook's Tip : Prawn balls can be used instead of pork balls.

savoury fritter starter

ingredients

300 gm cauliflower (cut into florets)
2 green peppers (sliced thick)
2 chinese eggplants (sliced thick)
2 boiled potatoes (sliced thick)
2 cups oil for deep frying
batter
300 gm chick pea flour
200 gm wheat flour
pinch of salt
water

method

Mix the chick pea flour, wheat flour and salt with enough water to form a thick batter. Leave aside for 30 minutes.
Dip vegetables into batter and deep fry until golden brown.
Dish out and serve with either sweet chilli sauce or hot chilli sauce.
Serves 2

Cook's Tip : Should the fritters become soft, refry in hot oil.
Reheating in a microwave is not suitable.

opposite page: peanut sauce salad (recipe on page 72); pappadam starters (recipe on page 96)

pappadam starters

ingredients

250 gm minced chicken or beef
2 green chillies (seeded and chopped)
1 large onion (minced)
3 cm piece ginger (minced)
1 large clove garlic (minced)
1 level tbsp curry powder
1 tsp chilli powder
2 large potatoes (boiled and cubed small)
1 tbsp cornflour (mixed with hot water to form a thick paste)
1 packet medium-sized pappadams
2 tbsps oil

method

Mix the minced meat with the curry powder, chilli powder and salt. Set aside.
Fry the onion, ginger, garlic and chopped green chilli in 2 tbsps oil.
When onion starts to brown, add the minced meat and allow to cook.
Add the potatoes. Keep stirring, and mash the potatoes into the mixture.
Add more salt if necessary.
Remove and allow to cool.
Soften the pappadams by dipping in water. Wipe dry.
Place a meat roll in the centre of the pappadam and fold it in half, sealing the edges with the cornflour paste.
Deep fry the pappadam rolls until crisp and golden.
Remove and drain.
Serves 4

Cook's Tip : This dish should be served immediately.

johor curry noodles

ingredients

dry noodles (boiled and drained)
1 chicken (1½ kg — cut into large
pieces)
400 gm mustard green (blanched)
400 gm beansprouts (blanched)
6 pieces dried beancurd (cut in half)
1 cup coconut cream
3 cups diluted coconut cream

blend together
20 dried chillies
15 shallots or 3 — 4 big onions
4 cm piece galangal
3 stalks lemongrass
1 tsp turmeric powder
4 cloves garlic
5 candlenuts or almonds
1 tsp full shrimp powder
3 — 4 pieces dried tamarind
2 tsps chicken granules
salt to taste
2 tbsps oil

garnish
fried onions
chopped coriander leaves
chopped green onions

method

Fry the ground ingredients in 2 tbsps of oil
until fragrant.
Then add the diluted coconut cream and
dried tamarind.
Next, add the chicken pieces and salt.
When chicken is cooked put in the coconut
cream and the chicken granules.
Next, add the beancurd pieces and turn off
the heat.

to serve
Put some of the beansprouts in a bowl and
add the boiled noodles.
Pour the curried chicken generously over
the noodles and top with the mustard
greens.
Garnish with fried onions, chopped green
onions and coriander leaves.
Serves 4

deserts

coco caramba

ingredients for pastry

2 cups all purpose flour
$1/3$ cup margarine
$1/3$ cup shortening
$1/4$ tsp salt
4 — 6 tbsps cold water

ingredients for filling

2 cups young coconut flesh cut into squares
$1/3$ cup cornflour mixed with $1/2$ cup young coconut water
$1/2$ cup evaporated milk
$1/2$ cup sugar

method

Sift flour and salt into a bowl.
Add shortening and margarine, sprinkle with water and mix with a fork. Roll into a ball.
Use half the mixture to line an 8" pie pan. Trim the edges.
Roll out the other half of the mixture and leave aside.
Fill the pie pan with the pie filling .
Cover the pie pan with the rolled out half of the mixture.
Cut slits near the centre. Seal and flute edges.
Bake in oven at 200 degrees Celcius until golden brown.
Serves 4

Cook's Tip : Brush the top with milk for a golden shine.

maize medley

ingredients

250 gm white bread
3 eggs
125 gm sugar
125 gm butter
$\frac{1}{2}$ cup coconut milk
$\frac{1}{3}$ cup evaporated milk
1 tsp vanilla essence
1 small tin creamed sweetcorn
a pinch of salt

method

Remove the crust from the bread and break into small pieces.

Beat the eggs, adding the sugar and half the butter. Mix well.

Stir in the coconut milk, evaporated milk, vanilla essence and salt.

Add the bread and leave to soak for 5 minutes.

Stir in the creamed sweet corn.

Pour the mixture into a greased heat-proof dish.

Dot the top of the mixture with the remaining butter.

Bake in a moderately hot oven until the pudding has set and the top is brown.

Serves 4

Cook's Tip : Serve with thick cream if desired.

banana blast

ingredients

4 bananas (sliced in half lengthwise)
40 gm butter
40 gm soft brown sugar
$1/4$ tsp ground cloves
$1/2$ tsp lemon juice
$1/2$ tbsp orange juice
2 cm piece fresh young ginger
red and green glazed cherries (optional)

method

Heat oven until moderately hot.
Cream butter and sugar.
Beat in cloves, orange and lemon juice.
Add ginger which has been peeled and finely diced.
Arrange the bananas on a well greased baking dish.
Spread the butter mixture evenly over them.
Bake for 10 — 15 minutes, or until the top is bubbling and bananas are cooked.
Remove from oven and garnish with cherries.
Serve at once.
Serves 2

Cook's Tip : Use small, sweet bananas only.

opposite page: fizzy tropical punch (recipe on page 114)

pam's delicious pudding

ingredients

400 gm bottlegourd (grated fine)
1 cup coconut cream
1 cup palm sugar (melted)
3 eggs
4 tbsps condensed milk
4 tbsps custard powder
120 gm butter
4 tsps sugar

method

Put the butter and condensed milk in a bowl and mix well until mixture is soft.
Beat the eggs.
Mix the custard powder with the grated bottle gourd.
Add the butter and milk mixture into this and combine well. Add the sugar and coconut cream.
Pour in the beaten eggs and mix well.
Add the melted palm sugar.
Place the mixture into a baking dish and steam for about 30 — 45 minutes.
Decorate with whipped cream.
Serves 4

Cook's Tip : You can use unrefined dark brown sugar instead of palm sugar.

sparkling summer paradise

ingredients

1 ½ tbsps gelatine
½ cup hot water
350 ml chilled ginger ale
3 cups canned mixed fruit
1 tsp lemon juice
2 tbsps sugar
5 glace cherries (sliced)
sprigs of mint
whipped cream

method

Mix the gelatine in hot water and stir until dissolved. Leave to cool.
Then, add the chilled ginger ale and lemon juice. Leave to partly set.
Stir in the fruit and cherries carefully. Leave to set.
Turn out and decorate with cherries and sprigs of mint.
Serve with whipped cream.
Serves 2

fruity dreamboat

ingredients

2 cans fruit cocktail
1 cup sugar
1 egg
1½ cups flour
1 tsp baking powder
½ tsp salt
1 cup brown sugar
½ cup chopped assorted nuts

method

Mix the fruit cocktail, sugar and egg.
Add the flour, baking soda and salt.
Put into a 9" x 3" greased pan.
Mix brown sugar and nuts, then sprinkle over the batter.
Bake for 45 minutes at 180 degrees Celcius.
To serve, cut into slices and decorate with whipped cream, sprigs of mint and cherries.
Serves 4

Cook's Tip : Cubed fresh fruit can be used to garnish instead of cream.

emerald sweet rolls

ingredients

pancake

300 gm wheat flour

1 egg (beaten)

a pinch of salt

300 ml diluted coconut milk (150 ml coconut cream to 150 ml water)

green colouring

3 screwpine leaves

filling

300 gm brown sugar or palm sugar

60 ml water

50 gm sugar

a pinch of salt

1 cup dessicated coconut

white sauce

200 ml coconut milk

2 tsps cornflour (mixed with 3 tbsps water)

a pinch of salt

method

filling

Melt palm sugar in 60 ml boiling water over low heat. When melted, add the white sugar, dessicated coconut and salt. Cook for 10 minutes, stirring all the time. Remove and allow to cool.

pancake

Sift flour into a bowl. Add the egg, salt and coconut milk slowly, stirring constantly. Add the colouring and allow to stand for 15 minutes. In a lightly greased non-stick frying pan, cook the pancakes for about 1 minute on each side.

sauce

Mix the coconut milk, cornflour and salt together. Simmer over low heat until sauce thickens.

to serve

Place 1 tbsp of filling on each pancake, rolling up folding in sides. Spoon sauce over and serve.

Serves 4

Cook's Tip : This can also be served for tea. Omit white sauce.

starlight express

ingredients

600 ml fresh honeydew juice
200 gm small grain sago
90 gm castor sugar
2½ tsp agar-agar powder
100 gm plain melted chocolate
100 gm whipped cream
honeydew balls (scooped from fruit)
green colouring
pinch of salt

method

Wash, then boil the sago.
Be sure to remove excess starch under running water.
Heat the honeydew juice, add the sago, sugar and agar-agar powder.
Allow to boil gently, then pour into glass bowls.
For the topping, pipe cream on the moulds, then place a honeydew ball on it.
Top with melted chocolate.
Serves 2 — 3

Cook's Tip : Caramel can be used instead of chocolate.

opposite page: starlight express

edwina's mango fluff

ingredients

3 egg whites
3 tsp gelatin
1 cup hot water
½ lemon (juice)
1 cup sugar
vanilla essence
whipped cream
passionfruit or mangoes

method

Add gelatin to hot water and dissolve.
Allow to cool.
Beat egg whites, add lemon juice and
sugar slowly.
Then, add gelatin.
Place in a buttered mould and freeze.
When set, place mould in hot water and
turn out.
Keep chilled for 1 hour.
Decorate with whipped cream and
passionfruit or mangoes.
Serves 4

ginger beer

ingredients

450 gm ginger (cleaned)
600 gm sugar
3 cm piece wet yeast
2 lemons or 15 small limes
¼ teaspoon nutmeg powder
4 cm piece cinnamon
10 cups water
½ lemon (cut into thin circles)
white of one small egg
shell of one egg

method

Cut the ginger into thin slices.
In a large pot put the ginger, sugar, egg white, egg shell, nutmeg powder, cinnamon and the water.
Boil for about 30 minutes.

Remove scum and egg shell that rises to the top.
Do not stir. Remove from heat.
Pour the hot mixture over the yeast and stir.
Add the juice of 2 lemons or 15 small limes and the sliced pieces of lemon.
Set aside to cool.
Strain the cooled liquid through fine muslin into a clean jar. Pour into clean bottles until three quarter full.
Use new corks to close bottles.
Tie the corks down to prevent the liquid from leaking.
Keep for five to six days.
Serve chilled with ice.

pineapple rhapsody

ingredients

2 cups chilled milk
1½ cups chilled pineapple juice
¼ cup sugar
1½ tsps lemon juice
½ cup cream
a pinch of salt
sprigs of mint for garnishing
6 drops peppermint extract (optional)

method

Combine and beat all ingredients until frothy.
Pour into tall glasses and garnish with sprigs of mint.
Serve immediately.

opposite page: pineapple rhapsody

scarlet princess

ingredients

½ cup agar-agar (soaked and pressed down)
4 cups water
red colouring
1 can lychee
rose syrup

method

Put the agar-agar and water into a pan. Bring to the boil, lower heat and cook until agar-agar is dissolved.
Strain through a cloth into a bowl. Colour it pink.
Cool. When set, grate the agar-agar, using a large grater.
When ready to serve, put two or three teaspoons of grated agar-agar into a glass. Add four or five lychees
Add syrup and top up with chilled water and crushed ice.
Garnish with sprigs of fresh mint.

opposite page: scarlet princess

fizzy tropical punch

ingredients

2 cans pineapple juice (chilled)
1 cup orange cordial
2 bottles soda (chilled)
2 bottles ice-cream soda (chilled)
2 bottles lemonade (chilled)
1 can pineapple cubes
slices of orange and lemon
sprigs of mint

method

Mix all the ingredients together in a large punch bowl.
Add ice cubes.
Garnish with sprigs of fresh mint and slices of orange and lemon.

suggested menus
dinner/lunch

BELOW ARE SUGGESTED MENUS FOR A PARTY OF 6

MENU A
1. SAVOURY FRITTER STARTER
2. CHICKEN VELVET
3. ASIAN PORK CHOP
4. STARLIGHT EXPRESS
5. SCARLET PRINCESS

MENU B
1. PEANUT SAUCE SALAD
2. EASTERN SAVOURY RICE
3. KOFTA CURRY
4. EGGPLANT PICKLE
5. CURRY LEAF SPECIAL
6. BANANA BLAST
7. FIZZY TROPICAL PUNCH

MENU C
1. PAPPADAM STARTERS
2. SPICY INDIAN SOUP
3. SELVA'S LAMB CHOPS
4. SPICY POTATOES
5. COCONUT RICE
6. EDWINA'S MANGO FLUFF

MENU D
1. SILVER AND GOLD
2. STUFFED BEANCURD SOUP
3. STIR FRIED BLACK PEPPER BEEF
4. EXOTIC PHOENIX VGETABLES
5. STEAMED WHITE RICE
6. SPARKLING SUMMER PARADISE

useful kitchen & cooking tips

1. Rub ground ginger over fish before deep frying to remove any fishy odour. Alternatively, you can soak the fish in milk or thick tamarind juice for 5 minutes, then wash and season.

2. When roasting meat, place on a rack and not in the roasting pan itself as cooking the meat in its own juices tends to toughen it.

3. If salad ingredients lack texture and are limp, freshen in iced water then add chopped water chestnuts.

4. Grease dish intended for steaming before use as it's easier to turn out the finished recipe.

5. When extracting coconut milk, use warm water instead of cold to yield more milk.

6. For the calorie concious, coconut milk can be substituted with skimmed or evaporated milk.

7. To prepare a quick sweet sour chilli dip, mix together one part chilli oil to 2 parts vinegar, fish sauce and a bit of sugar.

8. A tablespoon of ground, toasted coconut adds body to curries.

9. Sliced green chillies pickled in sugar and vinegar goes well with noodle dishes.

10. Chopped assorted nuts are an excellent garnish for rich soups or few ingredient salads.

11. When using bamboo utensils, always wet with water first to prevent burning (especially when using bamboo skewers).

12. Frozen cheese is easier to grate. Grease grater to prevent cheese sticking to it.

13. Only fresh ingredients should be used to cook food which is going to be frozen.

14. When using dried chillies, always seed or the curry will be too hot.

15. When cooking sour fruit, add a pinch of salt as this lessens the amount of sugar needed.

16. To make a flaky pie crust, add milk instead of water.

17. To prevent fruit from darkening, add the juice of half a lemon.

18. Sprinkle salt in the fry pan before frying meat to prevent oil from spluttering.

19. When rice is not cooked well, it is because the steam has been unevenly distributed.

20. Peel onions under cold running water or chill before peeling to prevent irritation to eyes.

21. Add bay leaves to stored flour to prevent weevils.

22. Drop in a few ice cubes when cooking soups or stews. The excess fat will cling to the ice. Discard.

23. Add salt to a salad only before serving as salt toughens the vegetables.

24. To keep cauliflower white, add milk when boiling.

25. When roasting meats do not open the oven door in the first half hour.

26. Do not use eggs which are cracked in uncooked dishes.

27. Vegetables keep longer in hot weather if wrapped in several layers of kitchen paper and stored in the fridge.

28. Keep stale bread in the freezer and use for puddings or fried sandwiches.

Agar-agar
A seaweed based setting agent available in satchets. Similar to gelatine.

Beansprouts
Shoots of the mung bean plant. Available fresh or canned.

Black mustard seed
Has more flavour and is ideal for curries, as compared to the yellow mustard. Best used after dry roasting.

Chick peas
Available fresh or canned. Used in salads and stir frys.

Coriander
Available as fresh leaves for garnish or dry seeds for curries. Substitute with chinese parsley.

Coconut milk
Extract from fresh or dessicated coconut. Substitute with canned coconut cream.

Dried prawns
Available in powder form. If used whole, must be soaked in water for a few minutes.

Dried shrimp paste
Should be grilled or fried without oil first. Very pungent flavour and should be used sparingly.

Egg noodles
Made from flour, eggs, water and salt. Available fresh, dried or frozen. When using dried noodles soak in water first.

Fennel
Substitute with aniseed.

Fish sauce
Made from fermented shrimp paste. Used in salads and spicy dishes. Bottled commercially. Use sparingly.

Five spice powder
A blend of anise, fennel, cinnamon, cloves and pepper. Used to give body and flavour to food.

Ginger
For cooking purposes only fresh root ginger should be used. Powdered ginger has an altogether different taste.

Garam masala
A blend of powdered black pepper, cloves, cardamons, fennel and cinnamon.

Hoisin sauce
Made from soybeans, sugar, garlic, chillies, salt and flour. It has a tangy flavour. Excellent for marinating meat when grilling or roasting.

Jaggery
Also known as palm sugar derived from palm tree — used extensively in deserts and sweets. Substitute with dark brown sugar.

Lemon grass
Aromatic bulbous base used to give curries a lemon flavour. Available in powder form.

Laos powder
Powdered galangal. If used fresh, skin and slice fine or blend. Ingredient in curries.

Mushrooms
Dried chinese mushrooms must be soaked in water before use. Dried sliced mushrooms are available in most oriental stores.

Oyster sauce
A blend of ground oysters, soya sauce and brine. Used in chinese stir frys.

Soya sauce
A blend of fermented soyabeans, wheat, yeast and salt. Used extensively in Asian food preparations.

Salted soya beans
Available bottled whole or in paste form. Use sparingly and rinse off excess salt from whole beans before using.

Tamarind
Sour fruit of which the pulp is mixed with water to extract juice. Use in proportions called for in recipes.

Tofu
Also known as beancurd. Pureed soyabeans sold in cakes or squares. Use fresh as it does not keep well.

Turmeric
Fresh or dried, used in curries for colour more than flavour. Saffron is entirely different and has a stronger flavour.

Water chestnuts
The bulbs of an aquatic plant. Texture is crisp, available fresh or canned.

index

Spice List

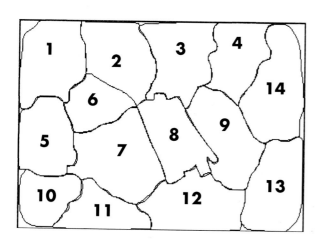

1 Fennel
2 Dried Red Chillies
3 Turmeric Powder
4 Curry Powder
5 Star Anise
6 Cloves
7 Cummin
8 Cinnamon
9 Coriander Seeds
10 Cardamon
11 Black Peppercorns
12 Poppyseed
13 Mustard Seed
14 Chilli Powder

This book is dedicated to my late father, **Joseph Pereyra,** who always told me that I
could do anything as long as I did it right .....

*a*sian spice
First published in Malaysia in 1998

by Ola Editions Sdn Bhd
20 Persiaran Wangsa Baiduri 7
SS 12, Subang 47500, Petaling Jaya
Malaysia

Text copyright ©
Joan Pereyra and Ola Editions Sdn Bhd
Design and illustrations © Ola Editions Sdn Bhd
Photographs © Ola Editions Sdn Bhd
Photographer : Michael Goh
Food Stylist : Terry
Designer : Morthy
Editor : T S Retnam
Publishing Consultant : Bernice Narayanan, BN & Associates Sdn Bhd
Printed in Malaysia by Syarikat Chan Brothers Printing
Colour Separation by PP Colour Scan Sdn Bhd .....

ISBN 983-99435-0-2